Sew Hot

in the Kitchen

18 Insulated Projects Perfect for Beginners

Abigail American Bennett

stash BOOKS
an imprint of C&T Publishing

Text copyright © 2020 by Abigail American Bennett

Photography and artwork copyright © 2020 by C&T Publishing, Inc.

Publisher: Amy Barrett-Daffin

Creative Director: Gailen Runge

Acquisitions Editor: Roxane Cerda

Managing Editor: Liz Aneloski

Editor: Kathryn Patterson

Technical Editor: Debbie Rodgers

Cover/Book Designer: April Mostek

Production Coordinator: Zinnia Heinzmann

Production Editor: Jennifer Warren

Illustrator: Aliza Shalit

Photo Assistants: Kaeley Hammond and Lauren Herberg

Photography by Estefany Gonzalez of C&T Publishing, Inc., unless otherwise noted below

Shutterstock.com photos:

Pages 2, 47 & 102: Africa Studio

Page 7: Fortyforks

Page 8: S_L

Page 9: Marcie Fowler - Shining Hope Images

Page 10 (bottom right): JollityFarm

Page 11 (top left): OlgaNik, EKramar

Page 11 (right): Stock High angle view

Pages 17 & 39: Photographee.eu

Page 19: travellifestyle

Page 23: Pixel-Shot

Page 45: Undrey

Page 59: Alena Ozerova

Page 61: vm2002

Page 99: united photo studio

Published by Stash Books, an imprint of C&T Publishing, Inc., P.O. Box 1456, Lafayette, CA 94549

Library of Congress Cataloging-in-Publication Data

Names: Bennett, Abigail American, 1992- author.

Title: Sew home in the kitchen : 18 insulated projects, perfect for beginners / Abigail American Bennett.

Description: Lafayette : Stash Books, 2020.

Identifiers: LCCN 2020023614 | ISBN 9781617459634 (trade paperback) | ISBN 9781617459641 (ebook)

Subjects: LCSH: Sewing. | Textile crafts. | Cooking.

Classification: LCC TT705 .B35 2020 | DDC 646.4--dc23

LC record available at https://lccn.loc.gov/2020023614

Printed in the USA

10 9 8 7 6 5 4 3 2 1

Dedication

To Daddy, whom I miss more with each passing day. I hope that the woman I've become would make you happy. This book is for you, Daddy. I love you.

To Paps. I can easily say that in my entire life, I've never looked up to a man as much as I look up to you. You encourage me, push me, believe in me, challenge me, and love me. I love you so very much and hope this work makes you proud.

To Koal—my favorite, my best friend, and honestly the sweetest most persistent man I've ever met. I don't know what I'd do without you. Thank you so much for being the kindest, most supportive man ever. I love you to the moon and back!

Acknowledgments

Special thanks to the following people:

My best friends and love-me-no-matter-what sisters, Apphia, Achaia, and Abiah. Thank you from the bottom of my heart for being my sounding boards and inspiration, and for always being there. Thanks for loving mac 'n' cheese, George Strait, and cowboys as much as I do. I'll love you forever.

My mommy—I love you. Thank you for showing me that anywhere can be home when you fill it with homemade goodness.

Nan and Paps, for constantly being there for me no matter what, loving me even though I'm a mess, and always being just a phone call away. I miss being there with y'all, but know I wouldn't be where I am today without your encouragement and guidance. I'll always be grateful. I love you with all my heart.

Mamaw Bennett, for showing me how to make southern sweet tea and for being the best mamaw ever. I love you.

Mamie and Papaw, for indulging my little girl heart with all the sewing supplies (and Wrangler jeans and ropes) I could handle at my tenth birthday party. Thank you for loving me like I was yours, because now you're stuck with me! I love you both.

Mama Erika, Dad Kreg, Kord, and Kash, for being my family. Thank you for asking about my book constantly and being just as excited as I was. Mama, for being my closest mom friend and for just getting me. Dad, for the calls while you're on the tractor and for letting me help out with the heifers. Kord and Kash, T-Bell runs at midnight with you two are my favorite. What would I do without you? Y'all are the bomb and I freaking adore you.

Mema and Boopa. Mema for being a part of this process, and Boopa for being so sweet and for taking me to breakfast. I love you both bunches!

Aunt Toogie and tribe, for encouraging me to write my next book. I love and miss your faces!

All of the amazing people in my life: my Texas family and friends, Uncle Eddie and Aunt Roseanna, Rhianna and Tyrel, my Oklahoma family and friends, my Indiana family and friends … I could go on forever. Thank you all for your friendship and for your encouragement as I went on this little adventure. Extra-special thanks to my heavenly Father, who brought me back to what really makes me happy.

Fat Quarter Shop and FreeSpirit Fabrics get a huge shout out for the amazing fabrics you see in this book! Without their kindness, it would've been harder for me to say exactly what I did with the designs you see here. If you haven't purchased their fabrics before, go do it *now*! You can count on their sweet and quick customer service and high-quality fabric. Tell them I sent you!

Roxane Cerda, Liz Aneloski, and all the amazing friends I now have at C&T for welcoming me back to the writing world and for encouraging me to take the route that's closest to home. This work came together seamlessly because of you.

Contents

8

36

CHAPTER 1:
What's in the Sewing Room 8

CHAPTER 2:
What's Cookin' in the Kitchen 18

11

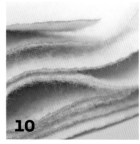

10

24

42

Introduction

Hey y'all! I grew up in a big family in which everyone and everything seemed to center around the kitchen and dining room. Even when Christmas dinner with the whole family required setting up card tables in the craft room, homemade pot holders and place mats found their way there, making the night that much more special and homier.

I love to be out and about, but deep down I'm a homebody. I'd rather be making you feel right at home with raisin oatmeal cookies or my mom's amazing manicotti served hot on a blue vintage plate and homemade place mat. Making Koal his requested biscuits and gravy, my father-in-law cookies, and my Paps his cup of hot coffee are really three of the things I love most. But it's not just the process of being in the kitchen that I love— it's the pretty things I use while I'm making my hearty tossed salad that really make me happy. It's the pot holder set that my sister made me for Christmas, and it's the place mats that my mom made when I was twelve years old that to this day find themselves on the dining room table at least once a week. Call me sentimental (oh, I am!) but it's something that makes me feel content and always will.

I've compiled some of my favorite kitchen, dining room, and food related things, including a few of my go-to recipes, all in one cozy book. Hot Cook Pot Holder Sets (page 20) are my go-to gift for housewarmings (let's face it—that pan is hot, but so are you). I like to make the Home Team Quilt and Cushion (page 76) for those fun game occasions but ultimately end up carrying the Let's Go Shopping Bag (page 66) to the bench with me. Because snacks!

So welcome to my kitchen and home! It's where we can all pull up a chair, prop up our boots, and snack on those warm snickerdoodles before the tacos are ready (I won't tell if you don't!).

I'm happiest here, and I hope you are, too.

XO,

Abi

CHAPTER 1
What's in the Sewing Room

Not everyone is going to have the same must-have supplies on their list, but I want to introduce you to the ones that I constantly go back to. I realize that some who pick up this book could be new to sewing (yay!), so I downsized the list to what's absolutely necessary. I don't want you to be mid-project and realize you're missing something.

Chewy Chocolate Cookies

Chocolate, anyone? Or maybe you're a peanut butter lover? I've got you covered! These are some of the yummiest cookies ever, and they're requested almost every time I offer to bring cookies to a party.

Ingredients

- 1¼ cups softened butter
- 2 cups sugar
- 2 eggs
- 2 teaspoons vanilla
- 2 cups flour
- ¾ cup cocoa
- 1 teaspoon baking soda
- ½ teaspoon salt
- 1 cup peanut butter chips

Directions

Preheat oven to 350 degrees F. Cream butter and sugar. Add eggs and vanilla. Stir in flour, cocoa, baking soda, and salt at one time. Once stirred completely, add peanut butter chips. Spoon rounded teaspoonfuls onto lined cookie sheet. Bake for 8–10 minutes. Cool on parchment paper.

Makes 4½ dozen cookies.

Must-Haves

▶ **Sewing machine**   Janome is my personal favorite, but I know my Nan is stuck on her BERNINA. If you are looking for a great purchase, I'd definitely suggest the Janome Jem Gold. It's a smaller machine, but it will do anything basic you could possibly imagine and has held up through many a project. It is still going strong today!

◀ **Insul-Fleece (by C&T Publishing)**   For this entire book, you'll need this product, and that's why it's listed in the must-haves. You can purchase this online from C&T Publishing (ctpub.com) in a package with a full sheet that measures 27″ × 45″. I usually grab 5 to 6 of these guys to keep on hand. Keep in mind what projects you're wanting to make right away and purchase the amount based on the projects. If you need larger pieces, it is available by the yard at various fabric stores.

▶ **Seam gauge**   While it's not necessary for every single project, I like having a seam gauge on hand when I need to be a little more precise with those measurements.

▶ **Scissors**   Good scissors can't be beat. Remember that. The sharper, the better.

▶ **Snips**   These small scissors are perfect for cutting those miscellaneous threads.

▶ **Seam ripper**   Mistakes will happen, but the seam ripper helps clear them out pretty quickly.

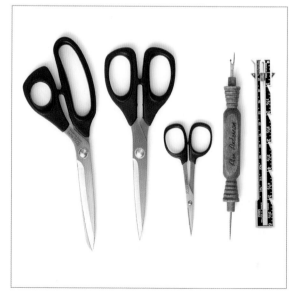

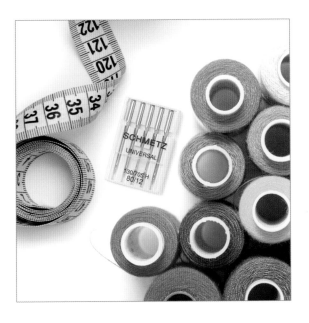

Sharp needles   I grab a whole set and go through them like crazy. Please—someone—tell me I'm not the only one who loses their needles! You can easily find them at your favorite fabric store.

Measuring tape   I keep a measuring tape and ruler with me constantly. Measure twice, cut once.

Thread   Go strong or go home! Thread is an investment for sure, but definitely worth it for the project outcome. Fraying doesn't happen and the stitches are stronger and look prettier, too.

Iron and spray bottle with water   Pressing the creases out makes your project shoot from okay to fab in just seconds!

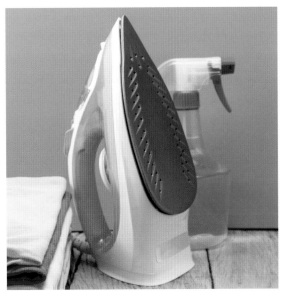

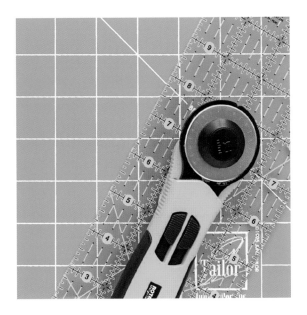

Cutting board, rotary cutter, and gridded ruler   A flat surface is necessary not only when you're cutting out your projects but also when you're creating your pattern pieces! A cutting board that's gridded will help make sure you're on the right track with straight lines for squaring things up.

Sewing with Insul-Fleece

As I stated before, this sewing book is unique because every single project features the amazing Insul-Fleece. This material, made of metalized Mylar, is layered with polyester fleece to create that high-quality perfection that reflects heat or cold and is surprisingly very simple to use. It keeps things hot or cold longer, which is why I love it in my Let's Go Shopping Bag (page 66). It works as a great filler and, once sewn in your project, can easily be washed and tumble dried on low with no bunching. The packaged piece measures 27″ × 45″, so I like to piece together Insul-Fleece as much as possible so I'm not letting any go to waste. It's not noticeable once your project is sewn up. Place the metalized Mylar side to the wrong side of your fabric, leaving the fleece side facing out. I've used the Insul-Fleece in a couple different ways. One is the obvious and above-mentioned heat resistance. I love this so much! It's simple but so necessary in the cooking and baking world. I mean, who wants to pull out a fresh pan of cookies and burn themselves in the process? Not me! That's why it makes sewing for the kitchen so convenient. On the other hand, you can use Insul-Fleece as a way to store heat, too. I use it this way in the Home Team Quilt (page 76) and Mama's Hot Rolls Towel (page 56). You can easily purchase this amazing material online from C&T Publishing (ctpub.com).

Please Note

Insul-Fleece *cannot* be used in the microwave due to the Mylar.

Insul-Fleece is heat resistant only—*it is not heatproof or fire-resistant*. Using an extra layer of cotton batting is recommended for pot holders. Use caution when handling hot surfaces with any insulated fabric craft project. Do not use an iron on the metalized Mylar side. Press on the fleece side only with your iron at the polyester or low-temperature setting.

Personalizing Each Craft

I'm a big gift giver. Giving, like sewing or cooking, is my way of loving. So if I give you something that has your name all over it, then girl, you know it's love. I do what I can to personalize whatever I give someone. I want that special person to know I was thinking of them and that I want them to feel it. When it comes to making the Table Spread Runner (page 52), Let's Go Shopping Bag (page 66), or maybe the Home Team Quilt (page 76), I always envision where my friend is going to be using it, how she or he is going to be using it, and more importantly what colors the home team wears! It seems like common sense, but I've found when my friend doesn't necessarily love the same things I do, I have to reevaluate but stick with the same game plan. I pay more attention to the colors and how she puts things together and also to where to find these colors and styles when I'm out shopping. Once you know how to make the projects like you want, it'll be that much easier to envision making them for your friend and them loving the results.

Fabric

When it comes to clothing, I will use almost any type of quilting cotton, voile, rayon, velveteen, knit, and so on. But when it comes to the kitchen, I strictly stay within quilting cottons and heavier material like home decor fabrics. When I'm feeling extra crafty or ingenious, I'll use a purchased dish towel. For projects such as Mama's Hot Rolls Towel (page 56), I'll use cotton on one side and a dish towel on the other side. This allows the towel to be a little more versatile and depending on how or where you'll be using the creation, it works! However, I would only suggest using towels for the projects where towels are specifically used as a fabric suggestion or option. Get creative and have fun. There are no boxes here, so feel free to go wild!

Your fabric choices also play a part in the style of your kitchen and home. The fabrics you choose will be out for everyone to see, use, and admire, but you want them to flow with the rest of your personal style so you don't end up unhappy with them. I have a lot of reds, oranges, blues, and greens in my little apartment. Although these fall under the category of my favorite colors, I continue to use these colors to keep things visually pretty.

Keep in mind the weight of your fabric. It is very important and often overlooked when people are rushing through the fabric store. (I get it—I've been there!) You can use heavy cottons in the Let's Go Shopping Bag (page 66), but you won't want to use something super heavy for Erika's Hot-Skillet Handle Cover (page 24) because it'll be more challenging when you're putting the cover together. If you want to try to make a project from this book with a different type of fabric, go for it, girl! Be sure and send me a picture, because I've got to see your beautiful work!

Wash your fabric before you start on any of your projects. Tumble dry low and use your iron like crazy. It makes all the difference in the world for your finished piece of art. I don't want you to finish your Set-the-Table Place Mats (page 48), run them through the wash for first time, and have them come out of the dryer all shrunken and puckered!

Just like the washing suggestion, I've got to mention that I've taken liberty with adding quite a bit of extra fabric for each project. This way there won't be as high a chance after washing, drying, and ironing your fabric that you'll be shy of what you need for the projects you've got planned. All yardage amounts are based on 40″ width of usable fabric.

Keeping This Simple

If you're a first-time sewist or just not that sure of your skill set yet, raise your hand! Friend, this section is all for you! I've been sewing since I was five years old. I was surrounded by it my entire life, and the only time I was ever unsure was when I turned eight and my mom decided I needed to learn how to follow a real McCall's sewing pattern. I wasn't okay with this. Yes, I wanted to know how to follow a pattern, but I loved doing whatever I wanted. I felt like having a pattern was a mix between downright cheating and having someone tell you what to do (not a fan of either). But I did learn, and that was the cutest apron I've ever made. I didn't realize that having the knowledge of understanding and following a pattern would open my eyes and creativity to a much broader field. Now I can glance at an illustration and get the project done. Sometimes, it only takes looking at the pattern pieces for me to get it right. I just don't want any of you to feel like I felt when I turned eight. What I'd love to do is walk you through some tips and tricks to keeping each project simple. I promise that if you get it wrong the first time, it's not a problem. I've been there too, and we'll figure it out together. Who's ready?

Cut out all your pieces first. Label them if you have to. I literally do this every time I make a quilt, and it's saved my biscuits more than once! Just make sure all pieces are accounted for and are the correct size.

Speaking of size—measure twice, cut once! I will never forget the time I laid that gorgeous piece of Jennifer Paganelli fabric out on the countertop. Y'all, I was stoked. I knew the exact skirt I wanted to make and how awesome it was going to look. It wasn't until I had finished cutting this cool skirt out that my sister Apphia walked in and told me that I'd cut the skirt out fine, but the fabric print was going the wrong direction! While she said it in the most matter-of-fact, kind way possible, it felt like she'd popped my balloon at my sixth birthday party. I was so sad but wanted that skirt so bad that I wore it with the design upside down anyway … partly because life's short, partly because I didn't have any more fabric. So "measuring" in the sewing world means checking off *everything*. If the pattern says, "cut on fold," make sure the piece is on the fold. It's nothing but common sense, but it helps to do a mental checklist so nothing is missed. That includes checking the direction of the fabric and of course making sure that the pieces are on the right side as directed. I lay everything out as I go and run through the pieces called for in the project before I even start sewing. This helps me get the project done faster and more effectively.

front panel

strap

I've already covered this a little bit in Fabric (page 13), but I feel like it's one of those things you can never say enough. Weight is so important. Be thinking about what your finished design will be doing. Carrying lots of groceries? Taking hot cookies out of the oven? Lying over the back of the couch? I love to mix my textures, but before I do that, I always take into account what and how I'll be using my finished project. If you want to go over what weight to look for when matching your pattern to fabric, go back to Fabric.

At the end of the day, it's all about how much you accomplished and how happy you are with your project, progress, skills, and how much you've learned. I'd love to see what all you do with the projects in this book, my first book (*Modern Prairie Sewing*, available in eBook only), or any sewing project. We're friends, and I care about my friends!

CHAPTER 2

What's Cookin' in the Kitchen

Ultimately, the kitchen is where we always ended up. The New Year's cheers at the island, teaching younger siblings how to roll out Great-Grandma Conwell's Christmas cookies, dancing and laughing with Koal in the kitchen, even dance-off sessions. They happened right there in the kitchen and remain among my favorite memories.

20
Hot Cook
Pot Holder Set

24
Erika's Hot-Skillet
Handle Cover

28
Tea Cozy

32
Trivet for Two

36
Bowl Cozy

40
Mug Rug

42
Warming
Veggie Sleeve

Soft Oatmeal Raisin Cookies

These are an unexpected crowd pleaser! I'm not a huge raisin fan, but these cookies are pretty darn good. They don't have too much sugar in them, either, and I love that. So yummy but almost on the healthy side! (I'm just being wishful at this point.)

Ingredients

½ cup softened butter

½ cup packed brown sugar

¼ cup sugar

1 large egg

1 teaspoon vanilla extract

1 cup flour

½ teaspoon cinnamon

½ teaspoon baking soda

¼ teaspoon salt

1½ cups old-fashioned oats

1 cup raisins

Directions

Beat butter and sugars together. Stir in the egg and vanilla. Add in all dry ingredients, raisins last. Stir. Chill dough for 30 minutes. Preheat oven to 350 degrees F. Drop dough by the spoonful onto cookie sheets that have been covered with parchment paper and flatten slightly. Bake for 10–12 minutes. Cool on parchment paper.

Makes 2 dozen cookies.

Hot Cook Pot Holder Set

Finished size: 8½" diameter

I love to give these as housewarming gifts! I also like to keep it fun by having different fabrics on both sides and really using my friend's personality as I choose my fabrics. This is one of my favorite starter pieces, too, for building on my home goodies. It's one of the first things I'll be using in my kitchen, and that's pretty exciting!

What You'll Need

- ⅜ yard of cotton fabric

- 1 package or ⅜ yard of Insul-Fleece

- ⅜ yard of 100% cotton quilt batting

- 1 package of extra-wide double-fold bias tape

Cut It Out

Cotton fabric: Cut 2 circles 8½″ diameter.

Insul-Fleece: Cut 1 circle 8½″ diameter.

Cotton quilt batting: Cut 2 circles 8½″ diameter.

Extra-wide double-fold bias tape

- Cut 1 piece 30″ long.

- Cut 1 piece 3½″ long for loop (*optional*).

Tips

I like to use a plate as a marking guide so my circle is nice and perfectly round. If your plate is wider than 8½″, remember to cut a longer piece of bias tape to fit around the edge.

Use this same concept but for a square pot holder. Cut out 2 squares 9″ × 9″ of fabric, 1 square of Insul-Fleece, 2 squares of batting, and 38″ of extra-wide double-fold bias tape. Follow the same instructions to complete the pot holder.

Instructions

Seam allowances are ¼″ unless otherwise noted.

1. Sandwich the circle of Insul-Fleece between the 2 circles of cotton batting and the fabric circles, with the right sides of your fabric facing out. Pin and sew around the edge.

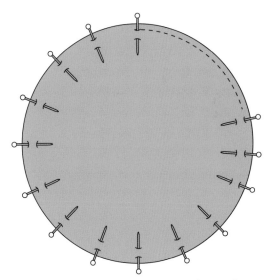

Sew main circles and Insul-Fleece circles together.

2. Open the double-fold bias tape and slip the raw edges of the pot holder sandwich inside the binding. Pin and carefully sew around the pot holder. At the end, fold over the raw edge onto itself and then cover over the starting point.

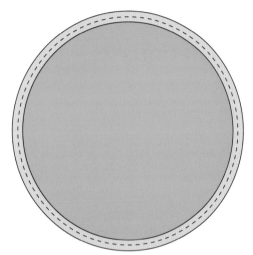

Finish raw edges with bias tape.

Tip For the round pot holder, gently press the 30″ piece of double-fold bias tape into a circle. It doesn't have to be the exact size of your pot holder but just enough to set the curve.

3. If you're planning to hang your pot holder, simply cut a strip of bias tape 3½″ long. Press each end under a scant ¼″; then fold it over where the bias tape meets on the pot holder and stitch in place.

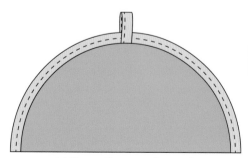

Add loop of bias tape (*optional*).

Erika's Hot-Skillet Handle Cover

Finished size: 4½″ × 10⅜″

It was a chilly Christmas morning in Oklahoma, and I was helping Mama Erika make biscuits and gravy. Everything was going great until someone decided to clutch the handle of the boiling-hot iron skillet, full of fresh gravy. I don't know what I was thinking, but if it wasn't for Mama, I would've ended up with a few more blisters than just the one I did! This project prevents blisters and is the only one in this book that I actually laugh over whenever I make it.

What You'll Need

• ⅜ yard of cotton fabric

• 1 package or ⅜ yard of Insul-Fleece

• ⅜ yard of 100% cotton quilt batting

Cut It Out

Cotton fabric: Cut 2 squares 8″ × 8″.

Insul-Fleece: Cut 1 square 8″ × 8″.

Cotton quilt batting: Cut 2 squares 8″ × 8″.

Instructions

Seam allowances are ¼″ unless otherwise noted.

1. Layer a batting square on both sides of the Insul-Fleece. Pin both squares of fabric right sides tougher; then pin them to the Insul-Fleece and batting layers. Sew around the edge, leaving a 2″ gap in one side. Clip the corners.

Sew all layers together.

2. Clip the corners and turn right side out. Push the corners out carefully. Slipstitch the opening closed. Press and topstitch around all sides ⅛″ from the edge.

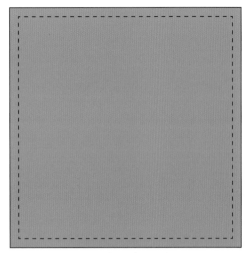

Topstitch ⅛″ from edge.

3. Fold over the right side ½″ away from the lower point and then fold the left to meet the right fold. Grab a needle and thread, and slipstitch together along the right edge, making sure to not catch the inside fabric. Knot the thread and bury the knot when finished.

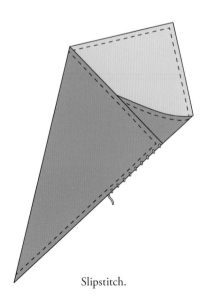

Slipstitch.

Tea Cozy

Finished size: 10″ × 14″

My family is from the South. Every Christmas, Thanksgiving, or birthday party had to include Mamaw's sweet iced tea. It just makes sense that hot tea, sweet cold tea, tea, period, happens a lot. This little tea cozy keeps the tea warm so your insides are always nice and toasty.

What You'll Need

- ⅜ yard of cotton fabric for outside
- ⅜ yard of cotton fabric for lining and loop
- 1 package or ⅜ yard of Insul-Fleece

Make the Pattern

- Trace the Tea Cozy corner pattern (page 31).

Cut It Out

Outside fabric: Cut 2 rectangles 15″ × 10½″. Fold in half and use the corner pattern to trim the top corners.

Lining fabric

- Cut 2 rectangles 15″ × 10½″. Fold in half and use the corner pattern to trim the top corners.
- Cut 1 rectangle 1½″ × 3″ for the loop.

Insul-Fleece: Cut 2 rectangles 15″ × 10½″. Fold in half and use the corner pattern to trim the top corners.

Instructions

Seam allowances are ¼″ unless otherwise noted.

1. Fold the loop rectangle's long sides in to meet each other. Fold over again and topstitch down the 3″ side. Fold and press the loop to make the shape of a *U.*

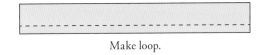

Make loop.

2. Fold one outside cozy piece in half and mark the center of the top edge. Pin the loop at the center top, matching the raw edges.

3. Pin both cozy pieces right sides together; then pin to an Insul-Fleece piece. Pin the second Insul-Fleece piece to the other side, keeping the fabric in the middle. Sew around the sides and top, leaving the flat bottom open. Clip the curves and press the seam to one side. Keep inside out.

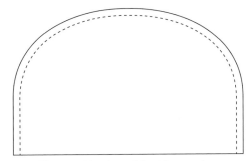

Place outside pieces right sides together, with Insul-Fleece on outside; sew curve.

4. Repeat Step 3 with the lining pieces only and turn right side out.

5. Right sides together, place the lining into the outside of the cozy, matching the side seams and nesting the seam allowances. Sew around the bottom, leaving a 3″ opening in one side. Turn right side out through the opening and push the lining up into the outside cozy. Slipstitch the opening closed and press the bottom edge. Press and topstitch around the bottom, ⅛″ from the edge.

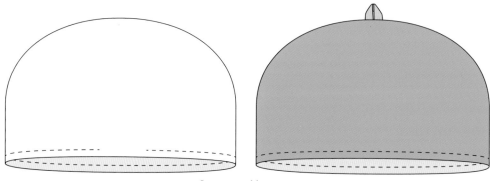

Sew around bottom.

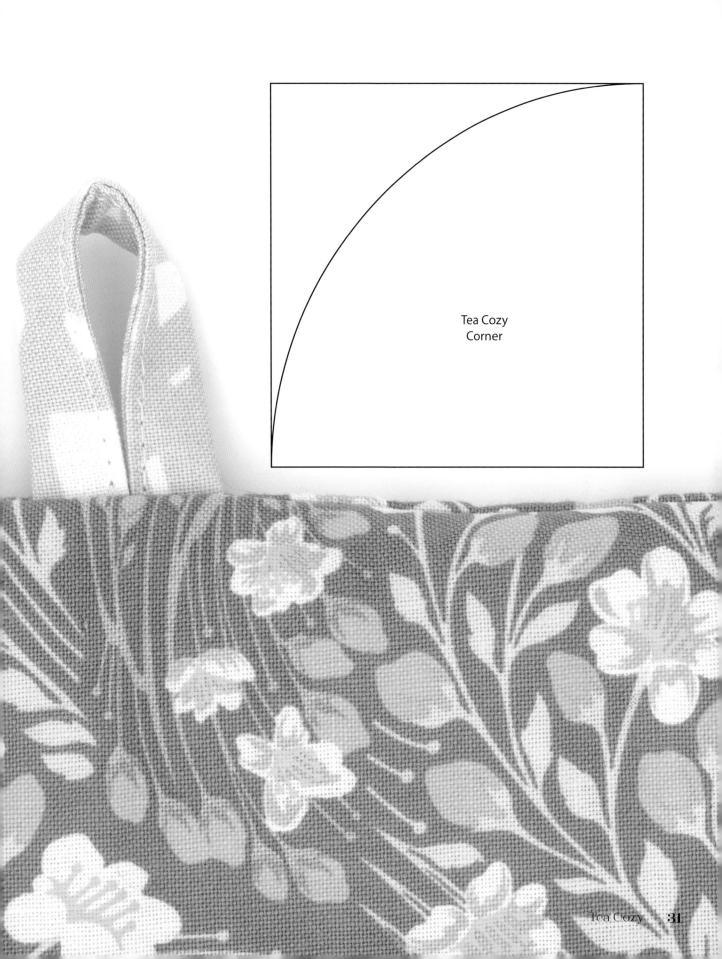

Tea Cozy
Corner

Trivet for Two

Finished size: 6″ × 6″

Trivets are my fancier version of my basic coasters. They are cute and slightly oversized, so they're perfect for those extra-big mugs. I can never get enough of sewing, and when it comes to my kitchen, I'm always excited to add something new to it. Thus Trivets for Two happened. You're welcome!

What You'll Need

- 3 cotton fat quarters (18″ × 20″–22″)
- 1 package or ¼ yard of Insul-Fleece

Cut It Out

Cotton fat quarters

- From each of 2 fat quarters, cut 2 squares 3½″ × 3½″ for the top of the trivet.
- From the third fat quarter, cut 1 square 6½″ × 6½″ for the trivet backing.

Insul-Fleece: Cut 1 square 6½″ × 6½″.

Instructions

Seam allowances are ¼″ unless otherwise noted.

1. Sew 2 squares 3½″ × 3½″ right sides together. Repeat with the remaining 2 squares. Press the seams open. Matching the seams, sew the units right sides together. Press the seam open.

Create patchwork.

2. Pin the patchwork top and the lining square right sides together, and then pin these to the Insul-Fleece square. Sew around all 4, leaving a 2″ opening on one side. Carefully clip all 4 corners and turn right side out.

3. Carefully poke all 4 corners out and slipstitch the opening closed. Press and topstitch around all 4 sides a scant ¼″ from the edge.

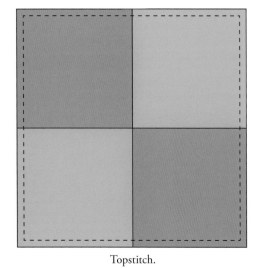

Topstitch.

Bowl Cozy

Finished size: 7½″ wide × 7½″ high × 3″ deep

Cowboy stew, comin' up hot! Keep it extra warm in this amazing bowl cozy. Don't feel guilty about setting the bowl straight on that perfect coffee table in the living room while you watch your favorite John Wayne movie. This cozy will not only keep the stew hot but also prevent any heat damage to the table!

What You'll Need

• 1 or 2 fat quarters

• 1 package or ⅜ yard of Insul-Fleece

Cut It Out

Fat quarters: Cut 2 squares 10″ × 10″.

Insul-Fleece: Cut 2 squares 10″ × 10″.

Instructions

Seam allowances are ¼″ unless otherwise noted.

1. Place the metalized side of an Insul-Fleece square on the wrong side of each fabric square. Sew together with a scant ¼″ seam allowance. Fold each square in half and mark the center of each side with a pin. Take a washable marker and flip over to the Insul-Fleece side. Using a ruler, mark a dot 2″ in from the center of each side. Measure ¾″ out from the center of each side and mark another dot. Draw a straight line from each edge dot to the inner dot. Repeat on all 4 edges of both fabric squares.

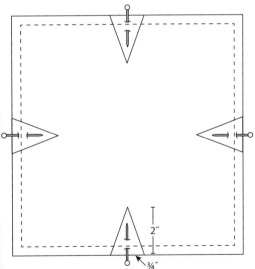

Draw darts on Insul-Fleece side of both fabric squares.

2. Fold one square right sides together at the dart and match the lines. Sew along the line and backstitch at the beginning and end. Repeat for all 4 darts in both squares.

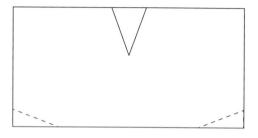

3. Right sides together, pin the cozy pieces together, matching dart seams and corners. Pin the darts to opposite sides for a flatter finish. Sew together and leave a small opening on one side for turning.

4. Carefully clip the corners and turn right side out. Push the corners out and slipstitch the opening closed. Topstitch around all 4 sides a scant ¼″ from the edge.

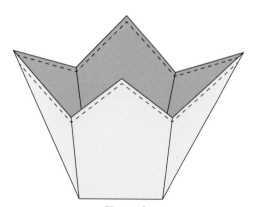

Topstitch.

Mug Rug

Finished size: 8″ × 20″

I like to throw this small convenient rug out on the coffee table, especially in the winter, when I know everyone's cup of hot cocoa or coffee is going to find its way to the living room. Make it out of pretty printed fabric so it flows with everything else in the living room, too.

What You'll Need

• 4 fat quarters

• 1 package or ¼ yard of Insul-Fleece

Cut It Out

Fat quarters

• From each fat quarter, cut 2 rectangles 3″ × 8½″ for the top.

• From one fat quarter, cut 1 rectangle 8½″ × 20½″ for the backing.

Insul-Fleece:

Cut 1 rectangle 8½″ × 20″.

Instructions

Seam allowances are ¼″ unless otherwise noted.

1. Arrange the rectangles 3″ × 8½″ in a pleasing order. Sew each pair together and continue sewing the sets together to connect all 8 to make the mug rug top. Press the seams open.

2. Pin the mug rug top and the backing rectangle 8½″ × 20½″ right sides together. Pin them to the Insul-Fleece rectangle. Sew together on all 4 sides, leaving a 3″ opening in one side. Trim the corners and turn right side out.

3. Carefully poke all 4 corners out and slipstitch the opening closed. Topstitch around all 4 sides ⅛″ from the edge. *Optional:* Stitch ⅛″ from each seam to quilt the mug rug.

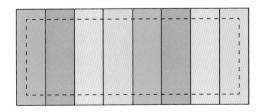

Warming Veggie Sleeve

Finished size: 8″ × 12″

This is perfect to store your veggies and keep them hot while you're prepping the rest of your meal. Pull your baked potatoes out of the oven and pop them in this little sleeve to keep them ready to eat.

Special Note

The Warming Veggie Sleeve *cannot* be used in the microwave at any time.

What You'll Need

- ⅜ yard of fabric

- 1 package or ¼ yard of Insul-Fleece

Cut It Out

Fabric: Cut 2 rectangles 8½" × 25" (1 for the outside and 1 for the lining).

Insul-Fleece: Cut 1 rectangle 8½" × 25".

Tip Make the Veggie Warming Sleeve the size that you need and want! If you're feeding a large crowd and want to keep all your baked potatoes hot, just cut out the size you'll need and follow the same directions. If you want sleeve to be more insulating, simply add another layer of Insul-Fleece.

Instructions

Seam allowances are ¼" unless otherwise noted.

1. Pin both rectangles of fabric right sides together; then pin to the Insul-Fleece rectangle. Sew together along the shorts ends only. Turn right side out. Press and topstitch the ends ¼" from the edge.

Fabrics right sides together, with Insul-Fleece on wrong side of lining

Topstitch the ends.

2. With the outside facing up, fold one end over 3½". Pin in place. Fold over the opposite end, overlapping the previous fold ¾".

3. Sew down both sides with a wide zigzag stitch, or use a serger if you have one. Turn right side out.

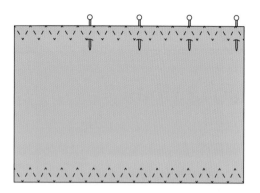

CHAPTER 3

Dining Room

Christmas dinners, the smell of freshly baked cookies coming from the kitchen, learning how to set the table with Mom's homemade place mats and napkins—it all happened there in the dining room.

48
Set-the-Table Place Mats

52
Table Spread Runner

54
Keep-It-Cool Coasters

56
Mama's Hot Rolls Towel

Nanny's Sausage Gravy

Ingredients

1-pound roll of ground sausage

2 tablespoons bacon grease or vegetable oil, if needed

⅓ cup flour, maybe a little more

3 cups milk, maybe a little more

Salt and pepper

Your favorite biscuits

Directions

Cook the sausage until done; then push it over to one side of pan. Tip the pan and see how much grease you have. If it's less than 2–3 tablespoons, I like to add some bacon grease or oil. Add the flour a spoonful at a time and mix into just the grease until a thick paste forms. Then mix in the sausage. Add a cup of milk and stir. Add another cup of milk and let bubble, continuing to stir. Continue to add milk until a nice thick gravy happens. The gravy will set, so add just a little more milk than you think you will need. Season with salt and pepper. Serve with flaky biscuits. Or on top of your baked potato. Or on your toast and eggs. It's that good!

Set-the-Table Place Mats

Finished size: 15½″ × 19½″

I'm pretty sure that as a kid I set the table 99 percent of the time. Don't ask my 3 sisters, because they might not agree with that. But I can tell you for a fact that we all had to say which set of place mats we wanted! Mom had about 20 sets (I might be exaggerating) in a vintage cabinet, and we'd rotate between our favorite sets. The bright floral was my favorite. Make a set of 4 or a set of 8 as your next housewarming gift!

What You'll Need

- ⅜ yard of main print for center (¾ yard for set of 4 place mats)

- ⅝ yard of coordinating print for border and backing (1⅝ yards for set of 4 place mats)

- 2 packages of Insul-Fleece (enough for 4 place mats)

Cut It Out

The cutting instructions are for 1 place mat.

Main print: Cut 1 rectangle 11″ × 15″ for the center of the top.

Coordinating print

- Cut 1 rectangle 16″ × 20″ for the back.

- Cut 2 rectangles 3″ × 20″ for the top and bottom borders.

- Cut 2 rectangles 3″ × 11″ for the side borders.

Insul-Fleece: Cut 1 rectangle 16″ × 20″.

Instructions

Seam allowances are ¼″ unless otherwise noted.

1. Sew the rectangles 3″ × 11″ right sides together to the sides of the center rectangle. Press the seams open. In the same way, sew the rectangles 3″ × 20″ to the top and bottom of the center rectangle. Press the seams open.

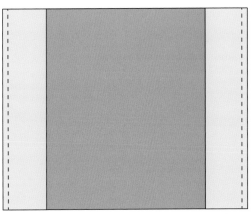

Right sides together, sew short rectangles to sides of the center.

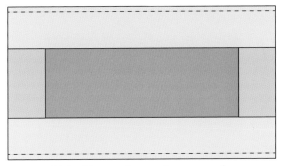

Right sides together, sew long rectangles to the top and bottom.

2. Pin the place mat top and backing right sides together. Then pin to the Insul-Fleece rectangle. Sew together, leaving a small opening on one side for turning. Clip all corners and turn right side out.

3. Carefully poke all 4 corners out and slipstitch the opening closed. Press and topstitch around all 4 sides a scant ⅛″ from the edge. *Optional:* Quilt ⅛″ seamline of inner border.

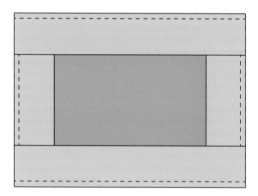

Tip: Make Your Own Napkins!

Simply cut fabric squares 14″ × 14″ and hem all sides. I press under ½″ on all sides and then fold the raw edge to the fold for a ¼″ finished hem. Homemade napkins are the best!

Table Spread Runner

Finished size: 18″ × length desired (The sample is 18″ × 70″.)

I love a good wooden table. Sometimes instead of covering it completely, I'll throw a pretty table runner down the middle. What's prettier than a clean, fresh runner and scent-filled flowers on the table on a spring morning?

What You'll Need

For longer runners, the yardage needed will be based on the length you desire.

• ⅝ yard of main print for runners up to 40″ long, using width of fabric

• ⅝ yard for backing

• 1 package or ½ yard of Insul-Fleece

Cut It Out

Main print: Cut 1 rectangle 18½″ × the length desired + ½″.

Backing: Cut 1 rectangle 18½″ × the length desired + ½″.

Insul-Fleece: Cut 1 rectangle 18½″ × the length desired + ½″. If the length needed is longer than the length of Insul-Fleece, piece the Insul-Fleece pieces by overlapping 2 edges by ¼″ and sewing together with a wide zigzag stitch.

Instructions

Seam allowances are ¼″ unless otherwise noted.

1. Pin both rectangles right sides together and then pin to the Insul-Fleece rectangle.

2. Sew around all 4 sides, leaving a 3″ opening on one side. Carefully clip all 4 corners and turn right side out.

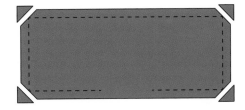

3. Carefully poke all 4 corners out and slipstitch the opening closed. Topstitch around all 4 sides, ⅛″ from the edge. *Optional:* Quilt as desired.

Topstitch.

Tip Add vintage trim or pompoms to the short ends of your runner to give it an extra-special flair!

Keep-It-Cool Coasters

Finished size: 4½″ × 4½″

Am I the only one that keeps a coaster on my nightstand? Please tell me you do, too! I scatter them on my table, in my family room, and even out in the garage. Too many coasters are like too many pillows—impossible!

What You'll Need

• 2 fat quarters (18″ × 20-22″), enough to make 8 coasters

• 1 package of Insul-Fleece

Cut It Out

The cutting instructions are for 1 coaster.

Fat quarters: From each fat quarter, cut 1 square 5″ × 5″.

Insul-Fleece: Cut 1 square 5″ × 5″.

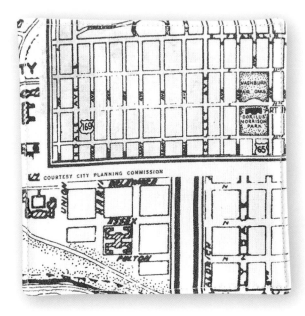

Instructions

Seam allowances are ¼″ unless otherwise noted.

1. Pin 2 squares of fabric right sides together and then pin to the Insul-Fleece square.

2. Sew around all 4 sides, leaving a 2″ opening in the middle of one side. Carefully clip all 4 corners and turn right side out.

3. Carefully poke all 4 corners out and slipstitch the opening closed. Topstitch around all 4 sides a scant ⅛″ from the edge.

Mama's Hot Rolls Towel

Finished size: 15½″ × 16½″

Fresh hot rolls out of the oven! Now, to keep them warm while the steaks come off the grill ... My sweet Mama Erika reminded me of this, and it made me think of the multiple times I'd cooked with my own mom. She'd use vintage tea towels to keep the rolls warm. I designed this towel that will not only keep those rolls warm but nice and toasty until you're ready to eat!

What You'll Need

• ½ yard of main print

• ⅛ yard of accent print for ruffle trim

• 1 dish towel at least 16″ × 17″

• 1 package or ½ yard of Insul-Fleece

Cut It Out

Main print: Cut 1 rectangle 16″ × 17″.

Accent print: Cut 1 rectangle 2″ × width of fabric.

Dish towel: Cut 1 rectangle 16″ × 17″.

Tip Depending on what kind of fabric the towel is made of, I like to take the leftovers and create a washcloth. Simply cut the towel down and hem the edges. These washcloths are my favorites and match the towels I use in my kitchen because they're literally the same thing!

Insul-Fleece: Cut 1 rectangle 16″ × 17″.

Instructions

Seam allowances are ¼″ unless otherwise noted.

1. Hem each long side of the 2″ accent rectangle by pressing under ½″ and folding the raw edge to the fold. Press again. Stitch along the inner fold. Fold the strip and cut in half.

---

2. To gather the strips, sew a long basting stitch down the center of each strip.

---

3. Gather each to match the width of the towel. Pin the first strip with the lower edge 1½″ above the bottom edge of the towel. Pin the second strip just above it, matching the raw edges to the sides of the towel. Stitch each gathered strip to the towel along the center of the strip. Remove the gathering threads.

4. Pin the dish towel and the main print rectangles right sides together and then pin to the Insul-Fleece rectangle. Sew around all 4 sides, leaving a 3″ opening in the middle of one side.

5. Carefully clip all 4 corners and turn right side out.

6. Carefully poke all 4 corners out and slipstitch the opening closed. Topstitch around all 4 sides ⅛″ from the edge.

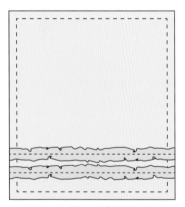

Topstitch.

CHAPTER 4

Out and About

I'm a firm believer in the fact that good times can happen just as much when you're out on the move as when you're at home. It's only natural that I make things for those occasions, too. So when I'm out running around, living my everyday life to its fullest, I have my home goodies with me. The Cold Beer Koozie (page 62) and the Potluck Superstar Tote (page 70) can both come to the same party and be helpful hits.

62
Cold Beer
Koozie

66
Let's Go
Shopping Bag

70
Potluck Superstar
Tote

76
Home Team Quilt
and Cushion

84
Bennett's
Lunch Bag

90
Snack Bag

96
Coffee Cozy

My Nan's Chili

Chili has always been a family favorite in my house. I remember as a little girl foregoing the turkey at the Christmas party and everyone grabbing a bowl of Nan's chili off the stove. People thought it was a weird exchange, but I just thought I was a cool kid and my family was awesome. Here's my spin on the chili recipe used back at the Christmas party of 1997.

Ingredients

1½ pounds ground beef

Seasoned salt

16-ounce can red kidney beans

15-ounce can ranch-style beans

16-ounce can chili beans

10-ounce can RO*TEL diced tomatoes and green chilies

46-ounce can tomato juice

Salt and pepper

1 tablespoon chili powder

Pinch of sugar

Directions

Brown the ground beef with the seasoned salt and drain off grease. Add all the canned goods and stir. Add tomato juice until you reach the desired consistency. Add seasonings, bring to a boil, and stir. Simmer until you're ready to ring the bell. Serve with tortilla chips, cheddar cheese, and sour cream.

Cold Beer Koozie

Finished size: 2⅝" diameter (fits standard beer cans)

This koozie will keep your favorite beer nice and cold. Feel free to have fun with them and decorate the cover to your heart's content!

What You'll Need

• ¼ yard of cotton fabric

• 1 package or ¼ yard of Insul-Fleece

Make the Pattern

• Trace the Cold Beer Koozie pattern (page 65).

Cut It Out

Cotton fabric: Cut 2 koozie shapes on the fold using the pattern.

Insul-Fleece: Cut 1 koozie shape on the fold using the pattern.

Instructions

Seam allowances are ¼" unless otherwise noted.

1. Pin both fabric koozie shapes right sides together and then pin to the Insul-Fleece piece. Sew the long sides, leaving both short sides open. Clip the curves and turn right side out.

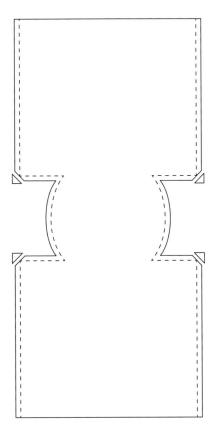

2. Fold the raw edges at one end in ¼″ and topstitch through all layers. Repeat for the other end.

Fold raw edges in; repeat on opposite end.

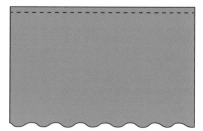

Topstitch both ends.

3. Fold in half, right sides together. Sew the side seams and turn the koozie right side out.

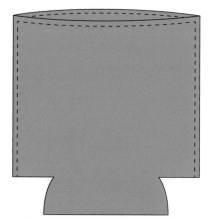

Sew side seams right sides together.

Cold Beer Koozie
Cut 2 from fabric.
Cut 1 from Insul-Fleece.

Place on fold.

Let's Go Shopping Bag

Finished size: 15½″ wide at top
(20″ wide at base) × 14″ tall × 5¾″ deep

I keep my bag in the car so when I do my random grocery runs it's ready to go!
It keeps the ice cream cold for the Fourth of July picnic or the rotisserie chicken
warm for supper. I don't think I'll ever be done making these for all my friends.

What You'll Need

- ⅝ yard of main print for exterior

- ⅝ yard of accent print 1 for exterior and handles

- ⅜ yard of accent print 2 for exterior

- 1⅛ yards for lining

- 1⅛ yards of fusible interfacing for handles

- 1 package or 1 yard of Insul-Fleece

Cut It Out

Main print: Cut 4 rectangles 9″ × 16″ for the outside bag.

Accent print 1

- Cut 2 rectangles 9″ × 16″ for the outside bag.

- Cut 2 rectangles 5″ × 37″ for the handles.

Accent print 2: Cut 2 rectangles 9″ × 16″ for the outside bag.

Lining: Cut 2 rectangles 17½″ × 29″. Stack the rectangles and measure 6¾″ in from the top left corner. Draw a line from this point to the lower left corner and cut on the line, or use a rotary cutter and ruler to cut the angled line. Repeat for the right side, so the top edge measures 15½″ and the base still measures 29″.

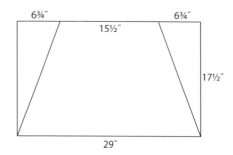

Fusible interfacing: Cut 2 rectangles 4¾″ × 36¾″ for the handles.

Insul-Fleece: Cut 2 bag shapes using a lining piece as the pattern.

Instructions

Seam allowances are ¼" unless otherwise noted.

1. Center the interfacing pieces on the wrong side of the handles 5" × 37". Following the manufacturer's instructions, fuse in place.

2. Make a handle by folding a rectangle 5" × 37" in half lengthwise and press. Unfold and fold the raw edges in to the center. Fold in half again and press. Topstitch both sides ⅛" from the edge. Repeat for the remaining handle and set aside.

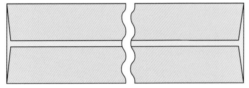

Turn raw edges in so they meet in middle.

Fold, hiding raw edges; sew both sides.

3. Create the outside bag pieces by arranging 4 rectangles in a four-patch, as shown. Sew together and press the seams open. Make 2.

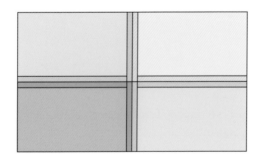

4. Using a lining piece as the pattern, trim each four-patch to the shape of the bag.

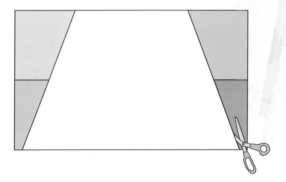

5. Pin each bag piece to an Insul-Fleece piece, and then pin the bag pieces right sides together. Sew together at the sides and bottom through all 4 layers. Press the seams open.

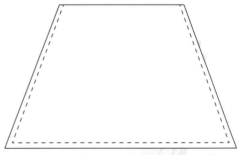

Sew outside bag right sides together at sides and bottom.

6. Make the boxed corners in the bag by folding the corners and matching the seams in the side and bottom of the bag. Measure 4" from the corner and draw a line perpendicular to the seam. This line will be 5¾" long. Sew along the line.

Trim the seam allowance to ¼″ and press the seams open. Repeat on the other side and turn the bag right side out.

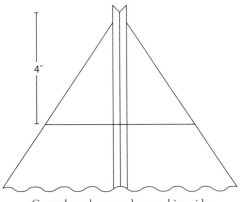

Create boxed corners by matching side and bottom seams and stitching.

7. Pin the handles to the outside of the bag, 2½″ from the side seams and matching the raw edges. Sew a scant ¼″ from the edge.

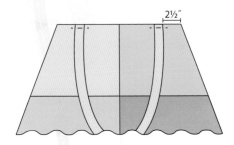

8. Pin the lining pieces right sides together, and sew the sides and bottom, leaving a 3″ opening in the bottom of the bag. Repeat Step 6 to make boxed corners on the lining. Push the outside bag inside the lining, right sides together, and pin the top edges together, matching the side seams and keeping the handles out of the seam. Sew around the top. Turn right side out through opening in the bottom of the lining. Sew the lining opening closed and press the seam open.

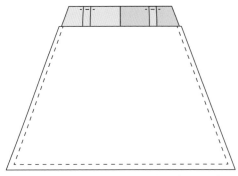

Put outside bag inside lining, right sides together.

9. Push the lining inside the outside bag. Press the top edge and topstitch around the top of the bag ¼″ from the edge.

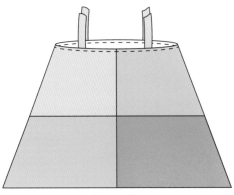

Topstitch.

Potluck Superstar Tote

Finished size: Fits 9″ wide × 13″ long × 2″ deep pan
and slightly larger

This carrier will hold that pan of deliciousness from your warm kitchen to the potluck while keeping it nice and toasty on the way. A cute pocket on the inside will hold whatever serving utensils you will need. Handles make it easy to not only bring the dish to the potluck but back home, too!

What You'll Need

• 1⅛ yards of main fabric for outside and lining

• 1 yard of contrasting fabric for pocket flaps and handles

• 1 package or ⅞ yard of Insul-Fleece

• 1¼ yards of fusible interfacing for handles (*optional*)

• ⅝ yard of ⅜"- to ½"-wide ribbon

Cut It Out

Main fabric: Cut 6 rectangles 11" × 16½".

Contrasting fabric

• Cut 4 rectangles 10" × 11" for the flaps.

• Cut 1 rectangle 7" × 20" for the pocket.

• Cut 2 rectangles 5" × 40" for the handle.

Insul-Fleece: Cut 6 rectangles 11" × 16½".

Fusible interfacing (*optional*): Cut 2 rectangles 4¾" × 39¾" for the handle.

Tip While fusible interfacing is suggested, you don't have to use it. I prefer to have the extra support in the handles because it's carrying my home-cooked dinner. I can promise you that my Mama Erika has one without interfacing, and it's held up just fine!

Instructions

Seam allowances are ¼" unless otherwise noted.

1. Pin and sew the Insul-Fleece rectangles to the wrong sides of all 6 of the outside and lining rectangles. Connect 3 of the rectangles by sewing the long sides, right sides together. Press the seams toward the center. Repeat with the remaining 3 rectangles. Press the seams toward the outside. Set aside one panel of 3.

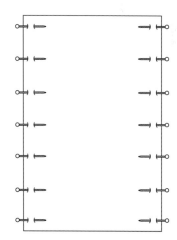

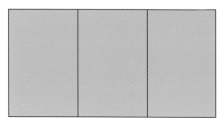

Make 2.

2. Fold the pocket rectangle in half to 7″ × 10″, right sides together. Sew the sides, clip the corners, and turn right side out. Carefully poke the corners out and press. Pin to the main panel 2″ from the edge. Sew down both sides of the pocket through all layers, ⅛″ from the pocket edge. Set aside.

Sew sides of pocket, clip corners, and turn right side out.

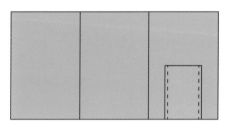

Sew pocket to main panel.

3. Cut the ribbon in half. Pin a ribbon strip in the center of the 11″ side of a fabric flap rectangle. Right sides together, pin a second flap rectangle to it, matching the corners. Repeat with remaining 2 flap rectangles and ribbon strip. Sew around 3 sides of each flap, making sure to catch the ribbons at the tops. Clip the corners and turn right side out. Carefully poke out the corners and press.

4. Right sides together, pin the flaps to the middle section of the remaining panel, matching the raw edges. Sew each flap in place.

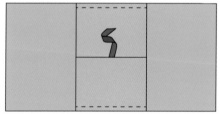

Sew the flaps to middle rectangle of panel,
right sides together.

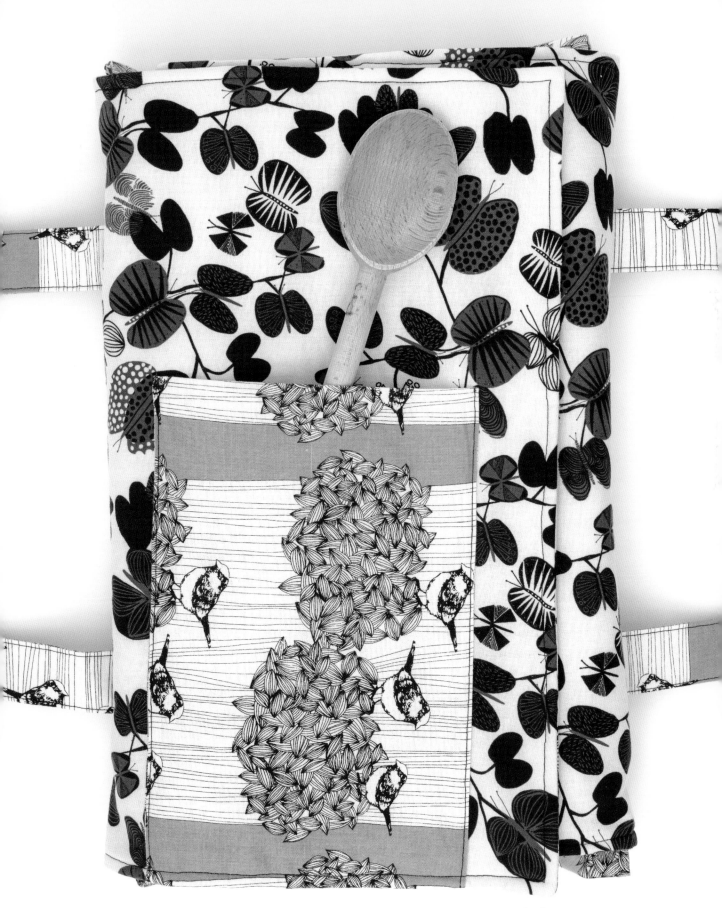

5. Pin the 2 main panels right sides together, matching the seams. Sew together, leaving a 4″ opening in the center of one side. Clip the corners and turn right side out. Carefully poke out the corners and topstitch ¼″ from the edge, being careful not to catch the flaps in the stitching.

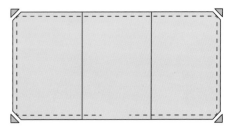

6. Center the interfacing pieces on the wrong side of the handles 5″ × 40″ and, following the manufacturer's instructions, fuse in place. Make the handle by sewing the ends of the 2 handle rectangles right sides together, creating a loop. Fold in half and press. Unfold and fold the raw edges in to meet in the middle, and then fold in half again and press. Topstitch down both sides, ⅛″ from the edge.

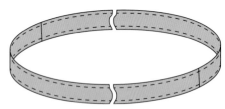

Topstitch each edge.

7. Open the carrier with the center outside panel facing up. Place the handle on the center panel, with the handle seams centered and the outside edges of the handle 3″ from the flap seams. Pin the handle to this center section only, and sew ⅛″ from each edge of the handle. Repeat on other side. I recommend using a walking foot to sew through all these layers.

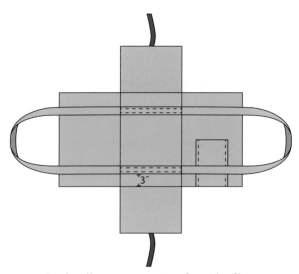

Sew handle to center section of outside of bag.

Home Team Quilt and Cushion

Finished sizes: 68˝ × 86˝ (quilt), 10˝ wide × 36˝ long × 2˝ deep (cushion)

Let's root, root, root for the home team! It's nearing halftime, and you're ready for more nachos and beer, but let's face it—it's chilly and your bottom's a little sore from sitting. Even the amount of time you stand on your feet, cheering the boys on, can't change the hard seat on those bleachers. With all this in mind, I put together this combo of both cozy blanket to keep you warm and a soft cushion for when you've had enough of the bleachers. The cushion folds in half and has a shoulder strap so your hands will be free to carry all the rest of your gear. Bring on the hot dogs; let's win!

QUILT

Tip If you'd like to make this quilt larger, simply decide how much bigger and buy yardage accordingly. To create a true twin, full, or queen, leave rectangles their full yardage width and then add enough rectangles to the bottom to make it the length you need. After you have sewn the rectangles together and your quilt top is complete, measure and trim as needed.

What You'll Need

• 1 yard of 6 different fabrics for quilt top

• 5⅜ yards for backing

• 1 yard for binding

• 6 packages or 4 yards of Insul-Fleece

Cut It Out

6 different fabrics: From each fabric, cut 5 rectangles 6¼″ × 34½″ for a total of 30 rectangles.

Binding: Cut 8 rectangles 3″ × width of fabric.

Instructions

Seam allowances are ¼" unless otherwise noted.

Hint I like to create a really fun, eye-pleasing combination for the top, making sure none of the same fabrics touch. I keep things playful with my home team colors but still cohesive enough that I can wash it off-season and throw it on my couch.

1. Arrange the 30 rectangles into 2 columns. Sew each pair of rectangles right sides together along a short end. Press the seams open.

Connect rectangles in pairs.

2. Sew the pieced rectangles right sides together on the long edges. Press the seams open.

3. You will need to sew the Insul-Fleece together to create a piece large enough for your quilt. If you are using the packaged Insul-Fleece, overlap the 27" edges of 2 pieces by ¼" and sew together with a wide zigzag stitch. Continue with the remaining pieces in the same way. Once all 6 pieces are connected in pairs, overlap the pairs along the 90" edges and sew together. If using yardage, cut

into 2 equal pieces and sew together along the long sides in the same manner.

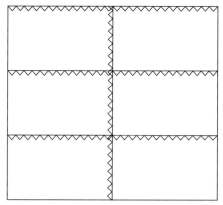

Sew Insul-Fleece pieces together, overlapping edges.

4. Cut the backing into 2 equal pieces and sew right sides together down the long sides. Press the seam open.

Sew quilt back pieces right sides together.

5. Lay the backing onto a flat surface, right side down. Hold tight and smooth with tape. Center the Insul-Fleece on top and lay the quilt top right side up.

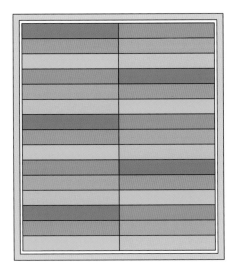

6. Smooth the quilt top and pin through all 3 layers using safety pins.

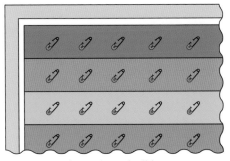

Pin baste through all layers.

Making It a Quilt

I love to take my quilts to professional longarm quilters. It makes the quilt that much nicer, and I love how clean the whole process is. It also gives me more time to work on other projects! But I also love hand quilting and the therapy that goes along with it. If you don't have a longarm quilter nearby and would like to get it done right there at home, I'd suggest the 3 different ways listed below.

Option 1: Hand quilt using a design that you've created. You'll notice that for my quilt, I simply followed the seams and stitched down both sides. It created the quaint look that I wanted and didn't take away from the beautiful fabrics I had chosen. Use sturdy quilting thread when you do this.

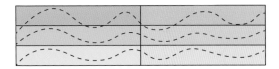

Option 2: Use cotton crochet thread and make knots throughout the entire quilt, going through all 3 layers.

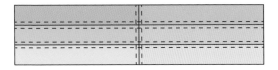

Option 3: Use your sewing machine! Start in the middle of the quilt and sew along the seamline. It creates a simple-looking quilt with a homey feel.

Finishing the Quilt

1. Place the binding strips right sides together at right angles. Sew the 8 strips together on the diagonal line. Press the pieced binding strip wrong sides together lengthwise.

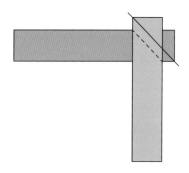

2. Place the binding strip on the front of the quilt, matching the raw edges. Sew onto the quilt with a ½″ seam. Fold the binding over to the back and slipstitch the binding to quilt around all 4 sides.

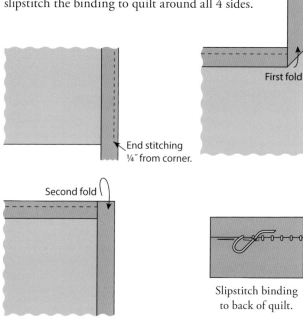

First fold

End stitching
¼″ from corner.

Second fold

Slipstitch binding
to back of quilt.

CUSHION

What You'll Need

- 1 yard of main print for base and handle

- 1 yard of coordinating print for cases

- 2 high-density foam pieces
  10″ wide × 17″ long × 2″ high

- 1⅛ yards of fusible interfacing for handle

Tip If you're purchasing a packaged high-density foam and you cannot find one that measures 10″ wide × 17″ long × 2″ high, simply purchase the one that's closest to those measurements. Mine were 10″ wide × 17″ long × 2″ high. Carefully use sharp scissors, an electric knife, or a blade to cut the foam. Do not do this around children or in a way that could possibly harm you. The foam doesn't have to be perfectly smooth on the edge, so I always suggest skipping the scary electric knife (unless we're talking about using it on the Thanksgiving turkey) and use sharp sewing scissors instead.

Cut It Out

Main print: Cut 1 rectangle 10½″ × 36½″ for the base.

Coordinating print

- Cut 2 rectangles 14½″ × 21¾″ for the cases.

- Cut 1 rectangle 4″ × 40″ for the strap.

- Cut 1 rectangle 4½″ × 10½″ for the center cover.

Fusible interfacing: Cut 1 rectangle 3¾″ × 39¾″ for the strap.

Instructions

Seam allowances are ¼″ unless otherwise noted.

1. For each case rectangle, cut 2¼″ × 2″ rectangles out of 2 end corners and 2″ × 2″ squares out of the other end corners.

2. Hem the 2¼″ short end of each case rectangle by pressing under ½″ and then pressing the raw edge to the fold. Stitch close to the inner fold.

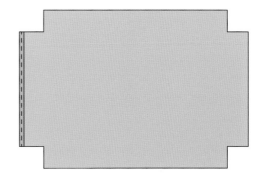

3. We want to create boxed corners on the case rectangles so the foam can fit into the cases as smoothly as possible. Fold the fabric right sides together at the corner and pin in place. The hemmed edge will be ¼″ shorter than the raw edge side. Sew together, stopping and backstitching ¼″ from the outside edge. Do this step on all 4 corners on both cases.

---

4. Pin the cases on the base, right sides together, matching the corners and with the hemmed edges facing towards each other at the center of the base. Sew in place, leaving the hemmed edges open. Press the seams to one side and press the raw edges at the center ¼″ to the wrong side. Turn each case right side out.

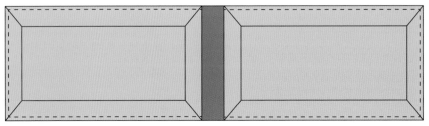

Sew cases to base, right sides together.

5. Fold the 4″ × 40″ strap in half lengthwise, wrong sides together, and press. Open and fold the raw edges to the center. Fold again and press. Topstitch ⅛″ from both long edges.

---

6. Press the raw edges of the 4½″ × 10½″ center cover under ¼″ on all 4 sides. Wrong sides together, center the cover between the cases and match the pressed edges. Pin all 4 sides in place.

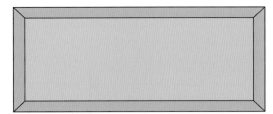

Press raw edges under ¼″ on all sides
of 4½″ × 10½″ rectangle.

7. Center one end of the strap under the center cover until 1″ is sandwiched between the cover and the base. Pin in place and repeat for the other end of the strap, being careful not to twist the strap. Sew all 4 sides of the center cover, stitching a square to reinforce each end of the strap.

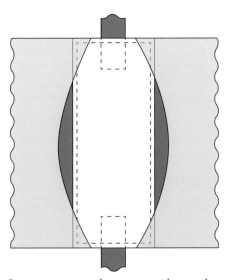

Sew center cover to base, wrong sides together,
and attach strap.

8. Carefully wiggle the foam pieces into the cases.

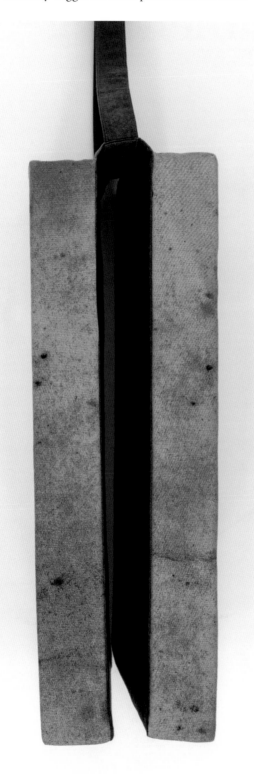

Bennett's Lunch Bag

Finished size: 10¼″ wide × 9½″ high × 3″ deep

Everyone needs a lunch bag at some point in their life—even my perfect two-year-old nephew, Bennett. But this is a little more fun than the basic lunch bags you can find in the store. I like to use camo fabric or bright, big floral prints just so I can make each bag more personable with my special person in mind. Slip in their favorite gooey peanut butter and jelly sandwich with a personalized note to make their day that much sweeter.

What You'll Need

- ½ yard of main print for outside

- ½ yard of coordinating print for lining and bottle holder

- ⅜ yard of contrasting print for handles

- 1 package or ⅓ yard of Insul-Fleece

- 12″ heavy zipper

- ⅜ yard of ⅜″-wide elastic

Cut It Out

Main print: Cut 2 rectangles 11½″ × 14″ for the outside.

Coordinating print

- Cut 2 rectangles 11½″ × 14″ for the lining.

- Cut 1 rectangle 10″ × 10″ for the bottle holder.

Contrasting print: Cut 2 rectangles 4″ × 22″ for the handles.

Insul-Fleece: Cut 2 rectangles 11½″ × 14″.

Tip Use oilcloth on the outside (and even the lining) for quick and easy clean-up. So many cute prints are available in this cloth! My nephew is only two years old, so even if he spills his milk or tips over his applesauce on his bag, it's an easy cleanup for my sister, who has two babies to care for.

Instructions

Seam allowances are ¼″ unless otherwise noted.

1. Pin a rectangle of Insul-Fleece to the wrong side of a main rectangle. Baste around all edges a scant ¼″ from edge. Repeat with remaining Insul-Fleece and main fabric rectangle.

Baste Insul-Fleece to wrong side of main bag pieces.

2. Pin the zipper to the top 14″ edge of the main rectangle, right sides together and centered. Stitch down the center of the zipper tape. Repeat to sew the other side of the zipper to the remaining main rectangle. Unzip the zipper halfway and pin the main rectangles together along the side with the top of the zipper only.

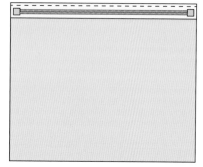

Sew zipper right sides together to bag's top edge.

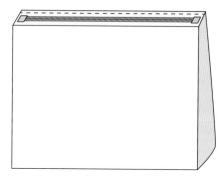

Repeat with remaining bag piece.

Sew bag pieces right sides together along the side with top of zipper.

3. Hem both sides of the bottle holder by pressing under ½″ and then folding the raw edge into the fold. Press and stitch each hem. Make casings for the elastic by pressing both the top and bottom under 1″ and then pressing the raw edge to the fold. Stitch close to the inner fold. Run the elastic through the casing with a large safety pin. Gently tug the elastic through. When the end of it reaches the very edge of the side, stitch in place. Pull the lead edge through, unpin, and stitch in place. Repeat these same steps for the bottom of the pocket.

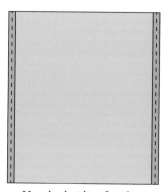

Hem both sides of pocket.

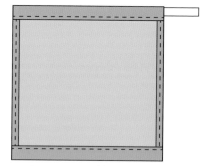

Create casings in top and bottom; run elastic through and stitch ends in place.

4. Open the zipper and pin the pocket to the side of the bag, centering it over the seam. Make sure to keep the pocket straight, with the top edge ½″ below the zipper seam and the lower edge 3″ from the bottom. Carefully sew down both sides close to the edge and again ¼″ from the edge. Stitch through the center at the bottom of the pocket so smaller drinking bottles won't fall through.

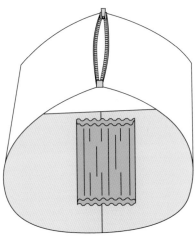

Pin and sew bottle holder to side of bag.

5. With the zipper open, sew the bottom and remaining side of the bag closed.

6. Box the corners by pinching the bottom and sides so that the side and bottom seams meet. Pin and mark at 3″ perpendicular to the seam. Sew on this line. Repeat on the other side of bag. Trim the seam allowance to ¼″. Turn the bag right side out.

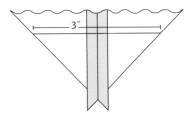

Create boxed corners in both bottom corners.

7. Make the handle by turning the long raw edges to meet in the middle, wrong sides together. Sandwich the raw edges in by folding over again and pressing. Stitch down both sides at ⅛″. Repeat with the remaining handle.

Turn handle's raw edges in to meet in the middle.

Sew down both sides.

8. Press the raw ends of the handles under ½″. Measure in 3″ from the sides of the bag and 1″ down from the top. Pin the handle in place, facing the raw tucked edge against bag. Sew in place. Repeat this step until both handles are secured to the bag.

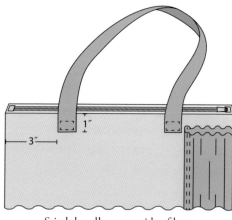

Stitch handles to outside of bag.

---

9. Place the lining pieces right sides together, and sew the sides and bottom with a liberal ½″ seam allowance. Create boxed corners in the lining by repeating Step 6. Press under ½″ at the top of the lining to the wrong side. Place the lining into the outside bag, wrong sides together, and pin around the top, matching the side seams. Carefully slipstitch the lining to the zipper on the inside of the bag.

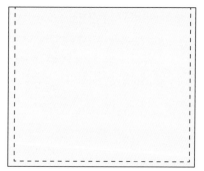

Sew 3 edges of lining rectangles, right sides together.

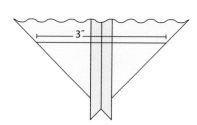

Create boxed corners in lining.

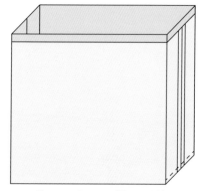

Press under top of lining ½″.

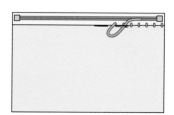

Slipstitch lining into outside bag.

Snack Bag

Finished size: 5″ wide × 10½″ high × 2½″ deep
(7½″ high when closed)

This is just a little smaller than Bennett's Lunch Bag (page 84) because snacks are always a good idea. A button-and-loop closure keeps this snack bag adorable and easily personalized. I decided to give an option for a wristlet handle so carrying your snacks is a little more convenient, too.

What You'll Need

- ⅜ yard of main print for outside
- ⅜ yard of coordinating print for lining, loop closure, and *optional* wristlet
- 1 package or ⅜ yard of Insul-Fleece
- ¾" button

Cut It Out

Main print: Cut 2 rectangles 9" × 13" for the outside.

Coordinating print

- Cut 2 rectangles 9" × 13" for the lining.
- Cut 1 rectangle 2" × 4" for the loop closure.
- Cut 1 rectangle 2" × 13" for the wristlet (*optional*).

Insul-Fleece: Cut 2 rectangles 9" × 13".

Instructions

Seam allowances are ¼" unless otherwise noted.

1. Make the loop closure by folding the rectangle 2" × 4" in half long ways, wrong sides together. Press. Fold the raw edges in to the center and fold in half on the crease; press again. Sew ⅛" from the edge. Fold and press into a U shape. Set aside.

Press raw edges to meet in middle.

Sew down the side.

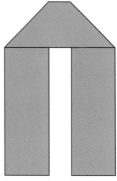

Fold and press in U shape.

If making the wristlet option, take the rectangle 2″ × 13″ and repeat Step 1, except do not fold into a U shape. Fold in half and pin at the side of the outside rectangle, 4½″ from the top.

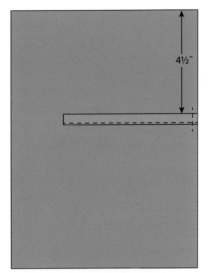

Optional wristlet strap

2. Pin the Insul-Fleece rectangles to the wrong sides of the outside rectangles and baste together with a scant ¼″ seam allowance. Sew the outside rectangles right sides together on the sides and bottom. To create boxed corners in the bottom of the bag, match the side seam to the bottom seam and pinch the fabrics together. Pin. Measure a line perpendicular to the seam that is 2½″ long and mark with a pen. Sew along this line. Trim the seam allowance to ¼″. Repeat with the other corner, and turn the bag right side out.

Sew outside rectangles right sides together, with Insul-Fleece on wrong sides.

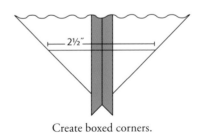

Create boxed corners.

3. Bring the 2 side seams together to find the center of the bag's top edge, and mark with a sewing pin. Pin the loop from Step 1 here and stitch in place. Set aside.

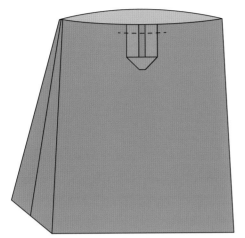

Pin and sew loop to right side of bag at center.

4. Take the lining pieces and sew the sides and bottom right sides together, leaving a 3″ gap in the bottom for turning. Repeat Step 2 to make the boxed corners in the lining.

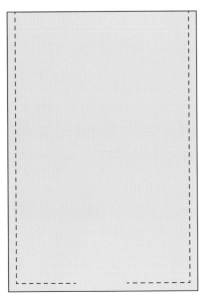

Sew lining pieces right sides together, leaving small space in bottom; make boxed corners at bottom.

5. Place the outside bag inside the lining, right sides together. Sew around the opening. Turn the bag right side out through the lining opening. Slipstitch the opening closed and push the lining into the outside bag.

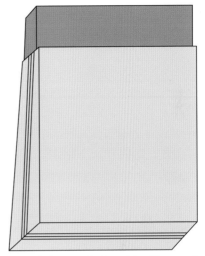

Put outside bag into lining, right sides together; stitch around top of bag.

6. Press the top edge and topstitch ¼″ from the edge. Fold the top of the bag over 3″ and make a mark on the bag front in the middle of the loop. Stitch your favorite button here.

Topstitch.

Sew button to front of bag.

Coffee Cozy

Finished size: Adjustable to fit up to a large coffee cup

Those tall mugs are always pretty cute and will keep your coffee nice and steamy, too. I like to add this cozy to personalize the cup that much more. As my Paps always said, "Coffee can never be hot enough!"

What You'll Need

- 1 fat quarter (18″ × 20″–22″)
- 1 package or ⅛ yard of Insul-Fleece
- 2 buttons ⅝″ diameter

Make the Pattern

- Trace the Coffee Cozy pattern (page 101).

Cut It Out

Fat quarter

- Cut 2 coffee cozies on the fold using the pattern.
- Cut 2 rectangles 1½″ × 3″ for the loops.

Insul-Fleece: Cut 1 coffee cozy on the fold using the pattern.

Instructions

Seam allowances are ¼″ unless otherwise noted.

1. Make the loop by folding the rectangle 1½″ × 3″ in half, wrong sides together, and press. Open and fold the raw edges to the center; fold back in half, and press. Topstitch ⅛″ from the edge. Press into a U shape. Make 2.

Turn raw edges in.

Sew down the side.

Form a U shape.

2. Pin the loops on the right side of the outside fabric piece, ½″ from the top and bottom. Sew in place.

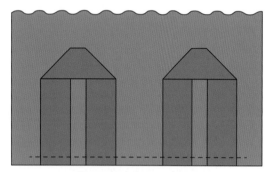

Pin and sew loops to cozy.

3. Pin both coffee cozy pieces right sides together; then pin to the Insul-Fleece shape. Sew around all sides, leaving a small gap in the bottom. Clip the corners and turn right side out. Press.

Sew cozy right sides together,
leaving small space open for turning.

4. Slipstitch the opening closed and topstitch ⅛" from the edge. Test the fit of the cozy to your cup and mark the center of the loops. Sew the buttons at the marks.

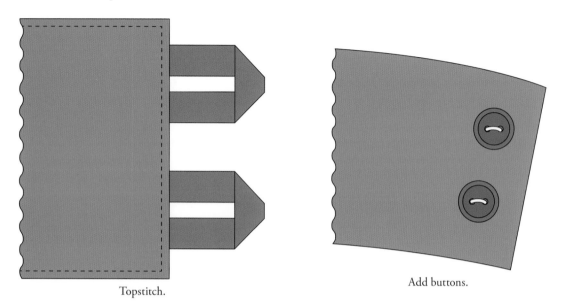

Topstitch.   Add buttons.

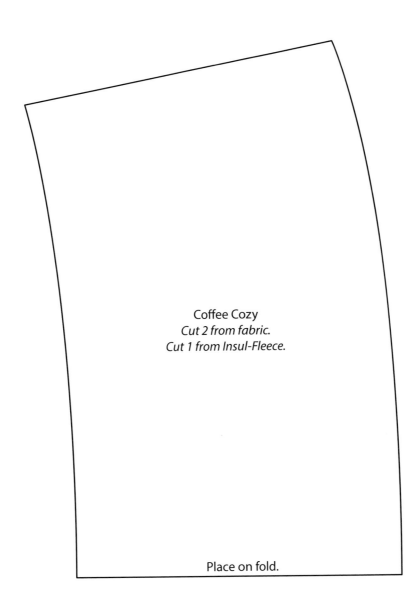

Coffee Cozy
Cut 2 from fabric.
Cut 1 from Insul-Fleece.

Place on fold.

Resources

These manufacturers continue to be my favorites and my first choices. While I tried very hard to stick with the latest prints, in hopes that you'd still be able to find them for yourselves, I can't guarantee that.

FreeSpirit Fabrics

freespiritfabrics.com

Michael Miller Fabrics

michaelmillerfabrics.com

Supplies

I go crazy over some beautiful fabric, and I couldn't have made this book without these amazing online stores.

Fat Quarter Shop

fatquartershop.com

Quilt Home

quilthome.com

**C&T Publishing
(Insul-Fleece)**

ctpub.com

FreeSpirit Fabrics

freespiritfabrics.com

About the Author

ABIGAIL AMERICAN BENNETT has been sewing and creating her entire life. She and her husband live in Fort Worth, Texas, with their dogs, Kowboy and Pistol. When she's not at work, she can be found in the Fort Worth Stockyards eating BBQ and getting a rack of longhorns with her husband and best friend, Koal Butler. If she's not there, she's probably at home creating something new in her sewing nook while homemade cookies bake in the oven. View her everyday projects and hair-coloring decisions on her blog. *Sew Home in the Kitchen* is Abigail's second published work with C&T Publishing.

Visit Abigail online!

Blog

abiamerican.blogspot.com

Also by
Abigail American Bennet:

Available as an eBook only